Bloodline is a mesmerizing, intelligent book, full of beauty, science, and ancestry. I love how it subtly weaves the threads of physics, nature, atomic destruction, and family into poems of great music and power. The figure of the grandfather—a physicist working on the Manhattan Project in a desert of blinding light and heat—is perfectly contrasted by the grandmother's world, a weightier mass of dark rooms and arid gardens. It's this contrast that brings the granddaughter's voice—and poetry—into the world. A poetry where one finds a comforting solitude out in nature. These are poems that I won't forget for some time.

—MICHAEL HENRY, EXECUTIVE DIRECTOR, LIGHTHOUSE WRITERS WORKSHOP,
NO STRANGER THAN MY OWN AND *ACTIVE GODS*

BLOODLINE

BLOODLINE

POEMS

::

RADHA MARCUM

THREE: A TAOS PRESS

Copyright © 2017 Radha Marcum
All rights reserved

First U.S. edition 2017

No part of this book may be used or reproduced in any form by any means, electronic or mechanical, including photocopying, recording, or any information storage and retrieval system, without prior written permission from the author, artist, galleries, museums, estates, and publishers.

Book Design & Typesetting: Lesley Cox, FEEL Design Associates, Taos, NM
Press Logo Design: William Watson, Castro Watson, New York, NY
Front Cover Artwork: The primary source of the LANDSAT False Image is LANDSAT, a USGS/NASA federal government program. Information, data, and images produced by this program are in the public domain and free of copyright claims.
Author Photograph: Erin Manning, Lafayette, CO

Text Typeset in Axiforma

Printed in the United States of America by Cottrell Printing Company

ISBN: 978-0-9972011-4-7

THREE: A TAOS PRESS
P.O. Box 370627
Denver, CO 80237
www.3taospress.com

For Doug, Isa, and Kieran

*And for Donald W. Mueller, Frances C. Mueller, and Edwin (Ted) Stein,
in memoriam*

CONTENTS

:: **BLOODLINE**

On the Half-Life of Facts	17
Fission, 1938	19
Technical Area 10, Los Alamos	20
Project Y	23
Letter, 1954	29
Wife of Classified, 1956	30
A Theory of Relativity	32
Oppenheimer's Dog	35
In the Making	36
Ninety-Four	39
A Physicist Remembers His Work	40
Elegy, In Reverse	41
Fragments	43
T'sankawi	45
Diving for Bells	48
His Ghost Returns to Frijoles Canyon	49

:: FAR FIRE

I.	Fireweed	53
II.	Prairie Grass and Cottonwood	54
III.	The Closed World	55
IV.	Twilight	56

:: RUMORS OF WATER

A Brief History of the West	61
West to East	62
Field in Drought	63
Winter Fire	66
Vignette for the Shortest Day of the Year	67
Empire	68
One Wilderness	70
Caddis	74

Notes on the Poems	77
Sources	81
Acknowledgments	83
In Appreciation	85
About The Author	87
Also By 3: A Taos Press	89

Thus memories, fragments of memories, lie, broken-edged, in the dark at the bottom of her blood.

—RAINER MARIA RILKE

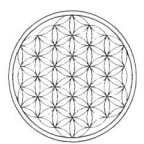

BLOODLINE

ON THE HALF-LIFE OF FACTS

My inherited skin is thin,
more purple than white, rough
paper on which some facts
spread tender, like pigment
bleeding in brushstrokes of water.
A useless plea bruises up
after news, from time to time:
*No more martyrs. No more
innocents.* New hates, old hates—
both fill us quickly,
like blood in a cut. Under one
banner they justify our errors while
from the brains' damp folds
continents bloom unceasingly
with the contents of events:
those who fled, those who
flee now. Once, in Krakow,
half a century after the last
great war, I watched as
hundreds of grackles shook
an old plane tree in the Planty
with terrible, blunt notes
until instinct rattled them and,
tremulous, they rose en masse
above us. No history seized
like a twisted kite string
in the crux of their hearts.
I loved the summer leaves
that replaced medieval walls
no less in knife-edge green,
no less the white water birds
circumnavigating trash
on the Vistula. Is it wrong
to wrest beauty from devastation?

Some facts have half-lives
so long they seem to leave
permanent bleeding beneath
the skin of cities. Smokestacks
and barracks; ashes descending
like birds on a fence of
densely planted trees; and,
behind an ordinary neighborhood
fence, the abandoned graveyard
where DNA ends, headstone
text obscured by the lush
unplucked plants rooted among
the dead roots of a race.

FISSION, 1938

Duet for Otto Frisch and Lise Meitner

It is like this:	It is not like this:
it is the clutch of	evidence crystallized by
winter in a Swedish village,	the morning before Christmas,
father in Dachau	post Kristallnacht and
the letter from Hahn with	shock of chemist's calculation—
barium from uranium?	on skis, over snow we puzzle it,
breath to breath, theory	by theory, fraction to fraction.
What is … is what?	Atoms from dead stars,
as old as Earth, and older—	the ticking Geiger counts
into a new era	nuclei not cleaved as expected
like a brittle solid	when bombarded, but pulled
like an elongated water drop,	surface tension, the
boundary unsustained with	electric charge, weakened. It is
a family of phenomena	with parts
hard to summarize as	existing inherently,
wave or thing—	releasing surfeits of energy
from a single atom	enough to make jump
a grain of sand,	and as we view
the Uranium nucleus	the human voice
(what will come	come what will)
breaks down	breaks down.

TECHNICAL AREA 10, LOS ALAMOS

for my grandfather, a physicist

Gray spider darts in contaminated lichens
where, in 1943, untethered from life

before the atomic split, you tracked
Bayo Canyon below the domestic

mesa tops, marked out this one spoke
of loneliness for the labs that began to radiate

in a half-web from the Jemez mountains.
Ideal for open-air experiments

on unstable elements.
Seventy years later, a barbed gatepost

still stands, unstrung and absolved of duties,
greeting the first female of your lineage

to take this path, a hummingbird sudden
like a bowshot across my back.

:

But what did I expect to find?
The bent tracks and metallic bits

of your radioactive experiments?
Remnants to explain

the spontaneous fission
of fear in a species that also believes

in Loaves and Fishes?
Not the spent coils of burned

bed-springs lit by some other's past
where lightning sometimes makes ghosts

of ponderosas and an unnamed red
wildflower disperses its trumpets

in pine duff.

:

For who among us doesn't
wish for our labors

to hold against the elements?

:

The canyon's throat
stays open and silent, except—

snip snip—a birdcall like scissors
cutting and cutting a notebook

to tiny, illegible scraps.

:

What do I choose
as my experiment? Temporary

containment in this narrow passage of oaks,
purple asters, red grasses above which

thunderheads grow by microseconds
more brilliant than any atoll test.

Soon they'll wear a burning dress
and bruise ash-blue, bottom-to-top,

shake loose the plumed-serpent water spirit
into a net of fleeting, mud-rich rivers.

The sky will beat the secret fragrance
from junipers and piñons

(you'll remember this)
like dust from a blanket.

PROJECT Y

Be tranquil in your wounds. It is a good death
That puts an end to evil death and dies.

—WALLACE STEVENS

Morning courtyard swept immaculate
with one feathered song—

Loretto Chapel inverted in my water glass,
placid on a surface that shimmers with voices.

March 23, 2013, Santa Fe, I write,
post-equinox, pre-Easter wind prevails

in the sheen of bare thorn-bushes
outside the Cathedral's silencing walls,

glance inwardly at this image.

:

Unbreakable glass,

which is to say, the post-graduate task
Grandfather undertook

as a scientist of practical physics
at Hartford-Empire

before he arrived here in 1943,
summoned by a paper

to Project Y, 109 East Palace.

:

Impregnated with hematite (iron oxides)
(element: Fe) the red mountains here

were named Sangre de Cristo: *Blood of Christ*.
I know the road by heart. The white crosses

of ordinary deaths marking the curves, atomic
Los Alamos cemented in swerving rows

on the Pajarito—*little bird*—Plateau.
This long slope (Christ's lacerated shoulder)

ends at the snowy lip of an ashen cup—
the caldera of a collapsed volcano.

:

We think we want it:
The Unbreakable, Incorruptible,

Immobilizing Science for a Predictable
Outcome. No happenstance.

But uncertainty conceives our shape
and makes our unmaking.

:

Just this, at the museum
in Los Alamos, near his
laminated black and white
Project Y identity (H-11):
A dusty, double-encased
specimen of green-blue Trinitite
collected from the test site.
Picture it from space: The gritty
iris of a dead eye, black center—
the massive, sea-flecked glass
blasted into the dark, pre-dawn
sand at the desert flat
on July 16, 1945. Ten seconds
of brilliant radiance witnessed
from a measured distance.
Leaning into the dimly lit relic,
its case reflects the photons
that cannot be absorbed
by this inherited face.

:

The reel no longer ticks, but in the museum
grainy pictures flash Reich and scientists,
marches and experiments, flags
and fragments of a context
so obliterated they cannot
reach critical mass.

Once, above Frijoles Canyon, I trespassed
on the chaotic midday sentences of black ants

tracking scent to the entrance of a tunneled depth,
each intruding grain carried out in their mouths

to where scraps of obsidian littered the ground—
sharp remnants of a culture that defended itself

with volcanic glass, then disappeared into the desert.

:

We are the glass blowers, the myth makers.
At the height of production, 70,000 atomic bombs
waited to make ash of the world.

I stare into opaque rocks, decode odd notes,
take broken and uncoiling shapes—the ghosts
of photographic evidence—into the wet

and changeable shapes of language. Like a pilgrim
to nearby Chimayo, I travel here to ingest the earth,
to contain sickness in a story.

:

Later, Oppenheimer spoke against the creation
of bombs 200 times more potent

than Hiroshima and was crucified.
My grandfather is still classified.

In love with The Mind of Science,
is our newest savior a cup without contents

or communion? What can I say to my children
when they find hollow, underground test chambers

in the dry, open spaces of their personal history?
Come. Descend with me into the round dark.

Reemerge from this kiva with the deity
the Hopi call *Másaw*—ash skeleton.

Let us rise from this crowded underworld.

:

One glossy thorn branch rakes the dry, yellow
Cathedral light. I write: *Mind on a precipice
in the leafless, finger-thin branches.*

Saints with Native traits, black and white eyes
and robes as bright as Mexican tiles, circulate.
Blood of Christ in fresh, ebullient red,

a Resurrection rich with pigment—orange cloak
rising over lapis stone. The Cathedral is a grove
of grieving. *Why is he bleeding?*

the lineage's latest Y chromosome asks.
Love, my husband says.
Love.

:

Love is the cup and what's
in the cup of the Last Supper.

Because we are breakable, we must
make our unmaking meaningful.

Almost Easter, I write, *wind makes
erasures, covers our mistakes.*

LETTER, 1954

Dear Object and Observer,

In living free, I have failed.
See Fig 1. Dandelion Explosions.
Fallout from last year's wishes
caught in the edifice of grasses

all across the just world
where our German shepherd pisses.
My wishes are misgivings.
To object is suicide,

as Teller tells it.
Whom do you serve? Dear
Eyes and Ears—jesters centered
in conscientious observations—

I implore you: *Hold mercy
in every nerve ending.* For this
I am a dog ostracized, an object
outside the never-ending

circle of Being, forever altered: O
O, and O in the gauzy field
of evening—dispersed rays
over the darkening world.

Humbly Yours,
J. Robert Oppenheimer

WIFE OF CLASSIFIED, 1956

Into the dry, electrical hum
of summer insects

smoke goes smuggling comfort
across her blood-brain barrier.

Four children in seven years,
in a house the second war built,

a family tree the arms race fed.
Grandmother: How rarely

she feels hunger as hunger,
in the stunned mechanism

of the two-beat flood, a beggar
at the gate of fiercer experiments

shut even to her, behind
his mind's guarded perimeter.

(After dinner it's the solace
of Wordsworth or *Scientific American*

alone.) So, at least grant her this:
smolder for the hive, a habit

to blunt the buzz of
sharper instincts. In time,

blindness. But for now, it's just
July, two decades before the first

grandchild arrives in this
enclosed carport where her ash-hand

sways as she squints to see
as the honeybee sees: in violent,

shuddering color. Here and there
in Grandfather's petunias, it takes

to the splayed crimson and indigo
throats that opened this morning

in brilliant photo-synthetic
ricochet.

A THEORY OF RELATIVITY

Bodies in motion
beget other bodies in motion.

Today off the cold mesa, light-waves
exaggerate the pines. Sand

anchors unlit candles in paper bags,
luminarias spinning still

with the Earth,
the old Plaza.

:

The speed of light is independent
of the reference frame.

But in the universe of no-absolute-rest
the actions of my mother's father

become a certain mass, pulling
our future off path.

:

In the experiment, a moving clock
runs slow to the observer.

If E = grandfather and his bicycle off to the lab,
then M is grandmother's abode, a mass

of tropical wood, burned
toast, earthenware cups, ebony

elephants marching up the baby grand,
its off-notes, the metronome.

:

Say you have this body,
then you don't—

you have time,
or you don't—

how will atomic history pull
on the rest of history?

Your children's children's children?
My children.

:

A moving clock runs slow
to the observer as a slowing mind

mocks its body.
In the next-to-last problem, after pissing

again in a neighbor's bush (his memory stripped)
he is shipped off to California where

one morning (consider the indirect sun, at an angle)
Mother asks me to solve a problem with salve

to pacify his cracked skin with ointment (tarry, black)
hence, a space-time equation I can't undo: the light

on his groin, shriveled
member of her begetting.

OPPENHEIMER'S DOG

Barks through all eternity
through piñon-wind and ether,
barks its piercing

harmonics from down
the dark block. Buries its bark
in my grandmother, my mother, me,

until memory splits its casing,
thrusts the old sound-bone—*regret*—
into the world once again.

With my instrument, I pick it up,
the inevitable.

:

Chases the wind through dry creek beds
and ochre canyons, on the mesas
and in bare, abandoned kivas.

Shakes the sound-post
of the family's cello, leaning
closet-dark in its sack.

Transmits its song
nevertheless.

:

Barks at the stars,
as over decades *regret* condenses
to a procession

of wind-lifted tears—flat, black seeds
arcing from the waterless yucca.

IN THE MAKING

> *But a kingdom that has once been destroyed can never come again into being; nor can the dead ever be brought back to life.*
>
> —SUN TZU

Suddenly cold, a shuddering rain
freezes our road a broken mirror—

Each day, I study the patterns
of dispersal, seed-heads released on a gust,

Grandfather's Los Alamos canyons
come to mind (his experiments, his

mind fused, unfocused
now). What are the networks,

the mighty dendrites,
trying to say?

:

What secrets, what
cased implosions, Grandfather,
what fission—was it all
nature's design? Now your brain—
what are we making?—
whispers bombs. The wind talks
a tin can flat. And after Hiroshima,
did you thirst, as we do,
for an undone God, the mind
like so many crows—burnt kindling—
suddenly floating?

:

In the field
of physics, fatality flowers

as *disintegration products*—
megatons of TNT—

lenses imploding
toward a volatile core

where *isotope*
fizzles in inert neurons,

a reference frame
of plaques and tangles.

:

The networks report that today
many (again, in our names)
were killed, incendiary.
At twilight, the aspen here burn
without burning—lights left on
accidentally in the grove.

:

Without effort, the laws of physics erase
the words for *moon sunk to its last horn-tip,*
erase another hundred faces.

For us, there isn't a day
the naming is enough: *Alzheimer's, nuclear
arsenals* (your truth fused, classified, secretly

detonated). Somewhere nearby, a neighbor drops
a box of tools. This morning, long ago,
my husband and I made love.

Poetry, like God (bomb, sarcophagus),
is just something beautiful to die inside.
Now, there go the geese—a fleet of facts,

of tiny hearts—pencil marks on their way.

NINETY-FOUR

All through his voice the thick
flakes fall—sentences broken between

poles—as wires shudder and shed their crusted
light. His mind is a melting ground, a naked

grange. Under the white weight
he remembers swimming elephants, listens

to *ifs* falling from the eaves. A shrike
settles in to pecking what wiggles

below the snow, and by his makeshift bed
I mumble *oh?* as he slips

across another forgotten pond.
Alone with the meadow's broken windows,

I watch the lawless heart of his abandoned
homestead molder, exposed—*who*

are you?—its stove cold
and full of mice.

A PHYSICIST REMEMBERS HIS WORK

The money I earned
from all the stars in the heaven ...

all the stars in the universe.
Does that make sense to you?

Mothers send their sons keys
in the piano, animals in the zoo.

You can look at these at your leisure
and give the results back to me.

You can tell me yes or no.
All of them are true.

You can say that all we receive,
all the light from all the universe

is one of the most astonishing of these things.
Flowers in the garden,

vegetables in the garden,
grass in the field.

ELEGY, IN REVERSE

Tepid sand, ordinary ash:
fire collecting smoke as flesh:

a lullaby back in the lungs
of his youngest daughter:

images reaffixed to consciousness:
a door with leaded Mexican star,

its light leaving the eye as
at a table his hand retracts

its slap from the child reaching
in innocent greed for berries:

and, further, a mountain chickadee's
see-saw song: and, further, the sea

backing out of the sea, hospital white,
fondling the twisted hood-ornaments

of pride and regret, the grit
that rises inside bloodlines,

in living rooms: from under glass
his children liberated

by brush from watercolor paper:
the lab's black and white photographs

disrobed, colorless as his wife's bed
before that blistered sky:

unimaginable light sucked into
the test tower:

and further back, eventually,
childhood's first experiment:

Who knew so much iron
existed in sand?

FRAGMENTS

for my grandmother

Because I can no longer see you on the mesa,
I take momentary faith in these four figures

and a mysterious fifth in background shadow,
this split-second exposure in which

Fermi, the great atomic scientist, and his wife
meet *Povi-cah*, Maria, the beloved Native potter.

Maria holds a bewildered grandchild
in her sturdy hands. Each beams brightly.

:

It took Maria and her family decades to temper
the right fire to create the famous black ware

gleaming with Wing and Storm, Corn Maidens, Rain—
pots that caught stray light on mantles, like yours,

of the scientists amassed above San Ildefonso Pueblo,
where the water cuts through.

:

Which images flashed inside you
after you went blind? Did you recreate the scene

of a wartime marriage—location undisclosed to us—
or the feathered feast-day dresses of pueblo dancers?

As I work with your fragments, they change
in me. They disintegrate like byproducts of fission,

you know, the ones they call *daughters*. They
coalesce in new forms, they radiate.

:

The light source in the photo is close—a window?
Window or not, their faces shine on one another,

this human being who identified the nature
of atoms in order to break them, and this artist

who gathered the ancient clay shards and made
a new beauty of that shattered past.

T'SANKAWI

As we are synonymous with and born of the earth,
so are we made of the same stuff as our houses.

—RINA SWENTZELL

In September, the blue grama straightens
before it bends its feathered knives to winter

and at last, once more, a downpour
pelts the mesa above the swift byways

of East Jemez Road and State Road 4,
deepens the vacant footholds of T'sankawi—

the village between two canyons
at the clump of sharp, round cacti—

uncovering these scattered parts
of pots that harbor the half-millennial dye

of human touch, where fingertips
coiled and smoothed clay, applied

a jagged black pattern and then
went on to the next task.

:

The scientists walked this circuitous path,
too, in 1944, breathless with war and formulations,

while in sumo halls hundreds of Japanese school girls
spread paper squares the size of road maps

to make fire balloons. They held no knowledge
of the purpose of their work, nor the secret

designs that would make *hibakusha* of us all.
Starving, they ate *konnyaku,* devil's tongue paste.

:

The element of earth was feeble in him,
said Rabi of Oppenheimer, yet

soles to stone stepladders, in silence bent
by a canyon wren or sharp wind,

near the scent of someone's den,
his mind took refuge here—

and Fermi, Feynman, Teller, others—
took refuge in its broken shapes

as I take refuge in the contours
of this poem, this place

where my bloodline was fixed,
for a time, no longer.

:

Did they survive, finding water's path
down to new food sources, or starve—

those who lost the diamond-shaped village
of T'sankawi to vagaries of sky?

It's uncertain. The curtain of rain lifts.
Water shadows the spotted faces

of petroglyphs down to the dark pits
gouged where the spirit emerges.

DIVING FOR BELLS

The dead are diving for bells at the bottom of the river,
are waiting in the ashes of robes,
are salt, are silt, are swallowing the ocean hours,
are walking a sunken road

wearing our imaginary clothes—

are knocking at your left ventricle,
are atoms rattling the bones of the stars,
are dreaming subnivean plants,
are coal-seam, wind shear, watermark

searing our nights with charts—

are falling like snow over red earth and glacier slough,
are cottonwood seed, sun-mote, tide,
cannot get over you,
are climbing.

HIS GHOST RETURNS TO FRIJOLES CANYON

To the creek and its snow-
choked wedding.
To sky-bare woods—
pools and drifts. To
slowing trout with
taut, watery bodies
hidden on carved rock.
To mossy isotopes of joy.
To the traces of ones
who cultivated dust—
vessels of reed
vessels of clay—
and left black, sun-flashed
flecks of arrowheads.
To fire-singed cliffs.
Here the Earth held
a man who seeded
a death flower, whose body
once-upon-a-time burned
with sun below
the abandoned caves.
Here he returns,
the summer's *musts*
laid down to *ifs*.
Only sparrows
shake the bush.

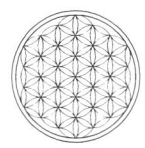

F
A
R

F
I
R
E

I. FIREWEED

        Clarity and then circumference,
the sun bent its thick

wheel across
        the unfenced ridge, across our

        blooming stalks—
and whatever we threw

windward, whatever
        we fought,

        still we multiplied
at the speed of small cities,

the rust
        of God.

        Undimmed, circling—
red-rock and

pine-scrub, the lure
        of everlasting longitude in

        the lit, silhouetted
grass.

Some of us knew fire.
        Some did not.

But whatever was severed from us
grew spires wherever

it went—
        while that far fire,

        heaven's hub, blended
the bent cities.

II. PRAIRIE GRASS AND COTTONWOOD

Celandine light, half-
life, the prairie whistles

this drought, snowless
gazes

        out of its tips.

        The sky cannot

come here—no, not a wisp
but starlings

shaking out of
cottonwood.

        Celandine light, half-

        alive—if it weren't

for this, for turning not
to water—

oh the prairie the mountain wait
for the sky to

        come.

        All afternoon the heart

drops notches
blue and then bluer.

III. THE CLOSED WORLD

Mid winter and the day-moon is
        button-holed

        in the west
in a sleeve of cloud-spill—horse tails

that wouldn't know
        the war of elements they are, come close—

        or the losses
that fill us, once and hence—snow

in the yucca pod,
        the terrible root of ice swelling

        down-canyon. Half
gray-eyed, asleep—*what returns us?*

Sharp glint against
        the damp-black mud—

        the door back,
contrast. Like all things,

a moment open, nothing less—
        cloud-shift,

        puddle, release.

IV. TWILIGHT

    Unmoored in a watermark—
dead ocean this country

depends upon—who can tell what
    survives? Not this

    jet-scratched sky. Not this
last puff

set into the pine shafts. What dark
    comes over us, like sugared water?

    What motor surging?
What moon plank?

Waterless wind makes its own song—
    tidy, temporal.

    Unmoored in dust—even the dust
a telling country. *No,*

it shifts, *way to know.*
    And so, *go to the river.*

    Trust me. I'll name the first star
forgiveness.

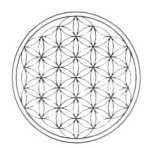

RUMORS OF WATER

A BRIEF HISTORY OF THE WEST

Like years, the desert
has no edges—red dust, red
dust condensed, busted ash—like years,
a corrupt uniformity we cut through.

:

Where miniature houses sail out
over shelves thrust up, where air breaks
down on rock, on conglomerate
that defines a sky.

:

Or dream dry salt seeps
from pores in your calves.

:

In one settlement, a headless
fire truck rusting by a shed, plastic
cowboys. In another, rancid
frozen confection.

:

One year, the lakes were too white
when we went by.

:

Where we go trailing
our own wake of glass, like years
we enter, enter again, stop seldom, and rest
in our own dust impressions.

WEST TO EAST

The bulbs refused to bloom this year.
In terms of relics, I fear, only dead things

are holy. Friendships. Snapshots.
Train tracks—oceans—crossed.

I tell you—so often, it's an eye
for all that the eye can see. No matter

who you are. All things set out from the earth
in a long shout. And you? Are you to market?

To marry? Look here, in this garden—
some small soul is anchored in a web

to the underside of a mask, one
that was always too small to wear.

FIELD IN DROUGHT

The seed is kicking in the earth.

—TOMAS TRANSTRÖMER

Dry daylight litters
the bitten shrubs, old pine cones

clustered in rock hollows, and the rocks
collected a century ago by some lonely homesteader

go on leaning into each other. Some grow cloaks
of neon-bright lichens.

:

The field undresses so slowly it seems
not to undress at all. The clouds

that hover and watch

are made of ice—are more like erasures
than water trucks.

:

From the field, memory emerges: On the far edge of Auschwitz, beyond the bombed crematories, seeking a quick exit by taxi, walking swiftly inside a barrier of perfectly planted trees, yards from the empty watchtower, we looked out at the usable fields where a child played in a plastic pool.

:

How naïve we are.
The knowable is always
relative to space and time,

scale and pace.
There are, after all, 20,000 species
of bacteria in the ecosystem

of the body, mine so dry
I've unconsciously scratched unreadable
red lines on one shoulder blade.

To my left, Bear Peak
hides thousands of thirsty heartbeats
in sandstone and burnt trees.

:

Snowless, the grass stands
mild and thoughtless, disorderly,

bent by ungulates.
That summer, the poet mistook our anxiety

for youthful longing—
Here, anxiety dries the desolate grass

to whispers. There is a rumor
of water amongst the cottonwoods.

:

In the windless sweep of pines,
a hawk's dive

makes the air sing involuntarily.
I touch the scratches *here*, as I walk

down the Big Blue Stem Trail.
It slopes out to the road

a few miles east where the sun-flaring cars
drive straight, accelerating

up the hill toward Rocky Flats so fast
that the grass and I

do not exist.

WINTER FIRE

You and I will go to the wild,
some day, without knowing
what has burned for weeks
uncontained—what smolders
yet by the smell of it
despite winter's best effort,
the snow. Flakes will fall on flame,
and drop by drop, water-thread
and rivulet, trace soot-lines
down glacier-carved granite.
We will taste it: acrid and bitter,
less of air and more of earth, the smoke
as viscous and reveling as the river
hissing and shushing under ice.
What illicit kindling
set this blaze? Which stranger
built a fire for a little warmth—
or the misguided comfort
of burning something?
And yet with tenderness
we'll stand in the many-eyed aspen,
unblinking, carved with adolescent loves,
while ahead of us a moose or elk
sets indelible parentheses
in the ash-dusted snow.

VIGNETTE FOR THE SHORTEST DAY OF THE YEAR

I broke time walking among the grasses, fractions
of papery stalks that traced and retraced circles

in wind-blown snow. I walked miles up the red canyon
channeling an iced-over creek like a worry soaked rag.

I asked the miniature cities of *equisetum* the secrets
they know. I asked the air pockets whitely flowing

under the ice what it was they carried—whose leafy breath
was confined therein. And I startled when a crow

choked on its own black thoughts as it flew along the facts
of wind-shift. Within the day, a new whiteness

would arrive in pines and pocked boulders. It sang
in the power lines lacing up the lonely woods. And I waited

in my smallest self with bright blood-flowering lungs
for the lion to leap from shadow, far on foot

from any witness. None came. Eight years I have lived
among these grasses. I saw not a soul

around the snowy back of Green Mountain
and felt light as a ghost released.

EMPIRE

Just under tree line
below the Continental Divide
the snow-crusted road swerves
where exposed rubble scrubs
interminable sky. As if
a great fire raged in the west,
ember-light glows on the topmost haunches
of earth while inside our tiny vehicle
we listen to a long-told story
about a real bird
and a mechanical bird,
and an Emperor visited by Death
who lives because he hears
once again the treasured song.
In the wild trees, beyond the far borders
of his garden, the little bird sang
with a voice like snow crystals
lifted by a long swirling wind.
How often do we choose
the radiantly jeweled thing
with innards like a clock,
when what makes us tick
is something plainer and stranger,
something terribly elusive
and infinitely joyful?

And we, in our sturdy and useful
vehicle, go on descending
the mountain, past the mine
that extracts a metal
that makes steel stronger.
After the tiny town of Empire,
a dozen ramshackle buildings
lit by neon Open signs, we join
the artery of brake lights above which
a single planet burns a hole now
slowly joined by more distant others,
some billions of suns
whose emissaries have traveled
so very long to reach us.

ONE WILDERNESS

We're weather.
What assembles never stays—

so many ordinary and small languages,
matter names, cell storms.

For instance, Our Lord's Candle
flowering white in the charred chaparral.

(Remember the man who couldn't rearrange
the ocean and so moved to the country

to move every rock from its place?)
What practice makes?

Windows. Also, stone seeds,
fire-broken cones,

and white water blistered
deep where the river's habit takes it.

:

Mid-trail, lizards mate.
A stamen-diving leopard lily
reflects on water-whorls
and backflow. Red mites,
manzanita, smooth stone
and the whole bank swim
to meet my creek-
concealed body.

:

Some days, the trail is clear.
But the trail also has fire bites

deep in felled wood,
and wild pea-vines

take us over.
What practice makes?

Attention to perpetual exoskeletons,
the lines defining a body.

Flies and fire ants. The way
a sudden yellow

water-snake curls in the mud,
in the stagnant path of river-shadow.

:

In the evening panes of attention,
a silk worm dangles
from a dark oak, slowly drawing up
its leaf-colored body
by swallowing an inner thread.
So a soul is said to be—asleep and
wandering—attached
to its body.

:

There are days
your feet disappear,

walking through a weedy drainage.
Days you disappear

in yucca spears
and granite.

:

Each morning, still attached—
though matter calls us *weather*.
Oak groves take us in, breathe
us out into sticky chaparral where
we are walking, walking
in and out a window of dust.

:

We're pilgrims.
As storms of flesh, we arrive.

(Remember the man who moved
to move?) Stones show a way

through a river to where?
We walk among black robes.

:

A long wind overtakes
the temple where we sit
every rock in its place.
Outside, mosquito clouds
find the warmth of other bodies.
What practice makes? Windows.
Also, words, silk threads,
these hands.

CADDIS

I lay a long time in the visual river,
between leaf-matter and the black rush, in a body-

cast of sand sinewed together. I let
the river into my house, into slits

in feathery gills, my wordless siblings stuck
to rock beside me. We lay between

what the river meant and what it means, its syntax
a tongue where our mother's wings dissolved

like rice-paper. Over and over,
light congealed in atom-strands of water; meanwhile,

God's motif hardened inside me—
first, the imprint of wings in loose molecules,

and then filmy wings. When I could stay
in and under no longer, the mirror

rivered itself and I flew
inside out.

NOTES ON THE POEMS

I have recreated events, locales, persons, and characteristics from my memories of them, family oral history, books, and other sources. However, many details are purely products of imagination and should be read as such.

EPIGRAPH

Rainer Maria Rilke, translated by Stephen Mitchell. Excerpt from "The Lion Cage," uncollected prose, *Ahead of All Parting: The Selected Poetry and Prose of Rainer Maria Rilke*. New York: Modern Library, 1995.

I. Bloodline

Poems in this section are inspired by the life of my grandfather, Donald W. Mueller, a physicist who joined Oppenheimer's Project Y (a sub-program of the Manhattan Project) in Los Alamos, New Mexico, in October 1943. In 1944, he met and married my grandmother, an adventurous and strong-minded Wellesley graduate originally from Maine. He joined the team tasked with developing the implosion design, which resulted in the first atomic bomb detonated near Alamogordo, New Mexico in July 1945. Conditions in Los Alamos were difficult for young families. After the successful detonation of Little Boy (over Hiroshima, a gun-design atomic bomb) and Fat Man (over Nagasaki, the implosion model) that ended the war, they moved their young family to Connecticut.

After the war, my grandfather resumed work at Hartford-Empire where he had previously conducted research on strengthening glass. However, they quickly returned to New Mexico, where he worked on Cold War nuclear warhead technologies for most of his career. Most details of his work remain classified. We do know that for some time he served as the head of the GMX-5 group that conducted implosion experiments in Bayo Canyon, known as "Technical Area 10," just two miles from Los Alamos. He and my grandmother remained on "The Mesa," with its rich geographical and cultural influences commingled with atomic research, until 1996. He died in 2004, at age 97, after suffering for 15 years with Alzheimer's Disease.

FISSION, 1938. Austrian-born physicists Lise Meitner and Otto Frisch (her nephew) together unlocked the mystery in Uranium experiments (performed in Sweden by Otto Hahn and Fritz Strassman), while each was visiting family in Kungalv, Sweden, during the Christmas holidays in 1938. Shortly thereafter, in January 1939, their findings were published as "Disintegration of uranium by neutrons: a new type of nuclear reaction" in the journal *Nature*. The news spread rapidly in the scientific community.

Physicists in the U.S., including scientists who had fled Europe, soon replicated and confirmed "fission," a term Frisch borrowed from biology where it is used to describe the process of a bilateral cell division—a life-sustaining process, ironically. This poem is in the form of a duet because the discovery was made collaboratively by the two relatives, as well as by Hahn and Meitner. And yet, Hahn alone won the Nobel Prize in Chemistry in 1944 for the discovery. Frisch gave piano recitals and played often on the Los Alamos radio station during Project Y years (1943-1945); the community referred to him as "our pianist."

TECHNICAL AREA 10 is a Los Alamos National Lab satellite site in Bayo Canyon, about two miles from downtown Los Alamos, and was the site of RaLa (Radioactive Lanthanum) implosion experiments. Bayo Canyon was called "Papa's Canyon" by his children.

PROJECT Y. World War II U.S. atomic weapon development was called The Manhattan Project. Under that umbrella, Los Alamos efforts became *Project Y*.

Frijoles Canyon, in Bandelier National Monument, is the site of Ancestral Puebloan ruins including tufa caves, a village, kivas, and farming remnants. *Chimayo*, a small town east of Los Alamos, is the site of the Sanctuario de Chimayo, built in 1813. Each year hundreds of pilgrims visit the Sanctuario to receive blessed earth, a purported cure for ailments of body, mind, and spirit.

Másaw is the Hopi god of fire, death, and the underworld (*Book of the Hopi*).

LETTER, 1954, is an imagined correspondence between J. Robert Oppenheimer and tribunal accusers. In 1954, Oppenheimer's security clearance was revoked by a tribunal of the Atomic Energy Commission for alleged association with communist groups. Although accusations were largely unfounded, Oppenheimer had in fact spoken out against development of ever-more powerful fusion bombs (H-bombs), developed in large part to show U.S. nuclear supremacy over the Soviets. Physicist Edward Teller was among those who testified against Oppenheimer.

WIFE OF CLASSIFIED. As the wife of a Los Alamos scientist, my grandmother knew next to nothing of what happened at the lab on a day-to-day basis. The level of secrecy that my grandfather's work required caused emotional distance and difficulty for his entire family.

OPPENHEIMER'S DOG. During the early years at Los Alamos, my grandparents lived near the Oppenheimers. My grandmother remembered hearing the Oppenheimers' German shepherd bark at night.

FRAGMENTS. The poem is inspired by a photograph (public domain, circa 1948) of atomic scientist Enrico Fermi and artist Maria Martinez. Martinez, with her family, became famous for recreating techniques to craft Puebloan artisan black ware ceramics.

T'SANKAWI is an historic Ancestral Puebloan site, part of Bandelier National Monument.

The epigraph is from Rina Swentzell, Santa Clara Pueblo architectural historian, in "Remembering Tewa Pueblo Houses and Spaces."

Hibakusha is a Japanese term meaning "explosion-affected people," as reported in *Hiroshima*, John Hersey.

Konnyaku is devil's tongue paste, a glue used to make balloon bombs, as reported in *Fu-Go*, Robert Coen.

THE DEAD. *Diving for bells at the bottom of the river* comes from a Hiroshima survivor's account published in *The Bomb*: An 11-year-old boy was playing "find the bell" with friends in the Ukrami River. He dove into the river to retrieve the bell just before the atomic bomb detonated over Hiroshima. When he surfaced, he heard his friends screaming in pain.

III. Rumors of Water

CADDIS. A caddis is a type of river fly whose larvae build tubular casings of sand and debris. They live on river bottoms in these open-ended sheaths until they grow wings, after which they live only a few days above water.

SOURCES

I owe debts of inspiration and fact-finding to the following museums, books, and articles.

Museums

The Los Alamos National Lab Bradbury Science Museum, Los Alamos, New Mexico.

The Los Alamos Historical Museum, Los Alamos, New Mexico.

Books & Articles

Church, Peggy Pond. *The House at Otowi Bridge: The Story of Edith Warner and Los Alamos*. Albuquerque: University of New Mexico Press, 1959.

Coen, Ross. *Fu-Go: The Curious History of Japan's Balloon Bomb Attack on America*. Lincoln: University of Nebraska Press, 2014.

Conant, Jennet. *109 East Palace*. New York: Simon and Schuster, 2005.

De Groot, Gerard J. *The Bomb*. Cambridge: Harvard University Press, 2005.

Hersey, John. *Hiroshima*. 1946. First Vintage Books Edition. New York: Vintage, 1989.

Mikesh, Robert C. "Japan's World War II Balloon Bomb Attacks on North America." Washington: Smithsonian Institution Press, 1973. Accessed via Smithsonian Libraries online.
http://www.sil.si.edu.

Rhodes, Richard. *The Making of the Atomic Bomb*. 2012. 25th Anniversary Edition. New York: Simon and Schuster, 1986.

Serber, Robert. *The Los Alamos Primer: The First Lectures on How To Build an Atomic Bomb*. Berkeley and Los Angeles: University of California Press, 1992.

Swentzell, Rina. "Remembering Tewa Pueblo Houses and Spaces." *The Multicultural Southwest: A Reader*. Tucson: University of Arizona Press, 2001; pages 86-90. Accessed via Google Books, July 2013.
[https://books.google.com/books?id= 8QRkz5 mo4XQC&pg=PA86&lg=PA86&d-q=remembering+tewa+spaces+rena&source=bl&ots=Z7X1hMPYoL&sig=I90tn-8cOS9pAbQhNdN6lmIt8wtM&hl=en&sa=X&ved=0ahUKEwjU6Y61tPzJAhUInYM-KHZ3zAKIQ6AEIKTAC#v=onepage&q=remembering%20tewa%20spaces%20rena&f=false].

Tzu, Sun. *The Art of War,* translated by Lionel Giles. Republished as an e-book by e-artnow, 2013.

Waters, Frank. *Book of the Hopi*. 1963, Viking. New York: Penguin Books, 1977.

ACKNOWLEDGMENTS

The author is grateful to these publications in which the following poems have appeared, some in other versions or with different titles:

Chelsea: "One Wilderness"

FIELD: "A Short History of the West"

Pacifica Review: "Fission: 1938" and "West to East" (which appeared under the title "Dear Tel Aviv")

Pleiades: "Caddis"

Poetry Northwest: "Fireweed"

Taos Journal of International Poetry & Art: "In the Making," "Prairie Grass and Cottonwood," "T'sankawi," "Twilight," and "Wife of Classified, 1956"

IN APPRECIATION

For wise counsel and encouragement, I would like to thank:

My husband, Doug Schnitzspahn, for suggesting the topic of this book and for his ceaseless faith in the poems that emerged.

Family: Elizabeth Mueller Marcum and Robert Marcum, Lynda Marcum, Kyffin Marcum, Deena Marcum Selko, Henry Mueller, Buffie Rosen, Karen and Leon Schnitzspahn, and Greg Schnitzspahn.

Fellow writers and readers, especially John Brehm, Rick Dickinson, Dana Elkun, Deborah Fryer, Buzzy Jackson, Carol Kauder, Hannah Nordhaus, Tracy Ross, Edwin (Ted) Stein, Michelle Theall, Rachel Walker, and Jeanne Yeasting.

And a very special thanks to mentors Veronica Golos and Andrea Watson of 3: A Taos Press, Linda Bierds, Steven Cramer, Richard Kenney, and Roland Merullo.

ABOUT THE AUTHOR

Radha Marcum is a graduate of the University of Washington, Seattle, MFA program where she held the Klepser Fellowship in Poetry. A lifetime explorer of the desert Southwest and longtime resident of Colorado, she finds greatest inspiration in the natural landscapes, history, and people of the American West. She has led creative writing classes in Seattle, Boulder, and Rome, Italy, and currently teaches at the Lighthouse Writers Workshop in Denver. Her poems, including some not collected here, have appeared in a wide variety of literary journals. This is her first collection.

ALSO BY 3:A TAOS PRESS

Collecting Life: Poets on Objects Known and Imagined
Madelyn Garner and Andrea Watson

Seven
Sheryl Luna

The Luminosity
Bonnie Rose Marcus

Trembling in the Bones: A Commemorative Edition
Eleanor Swanson

3 A.M.
Phyllis Hotch

Ears of Corn: Listen
Max Early

Elemental
Bill Brown

Rootwork
Veronica Golos

Farolito
Karen S. Córdova

Godwit
Eva Hooker

The Ledgerbook
William S. Barnes

The Mistress
Catherine Strisik

Library of Small Happiness
Leslie Ullman

Day of Clean Brightness
Jane Lin